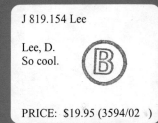

P9-CAP-724

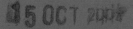

15 OCT 2007

DENNIS LEE

Illustrations by MARYANN KOVALSKI

KEY PORTER BOOKS

Library and Archives Canada Cataloguing in Publication

Lee, Dennis, 1939–
        So cool / Dennis Lee ; illustrations by Maryann Kovalski.

Poems.
ISBN 1-55263-613-5

I. Title.

PS8523.E3S6 2004   jC811'.54   C2004-903844-3

THE CANADA COUNCIL | LE CONSEIL DES ARTS
    FOR THE ARTS | DU CANADA

ONTARIO ARTS COUNCIL
CONSEIL DES ARTS DE L'ONTARIO

The publisher gratefully acknowledges the support of the Canada Council for the Arts and the Ontario Arts Council for its publishing program. We acknowledge the support of the Government of Ontario through the Ontario Media Development Corporation's Ontario Book Initiative.

We acknowledge the financial support of the Government of Canada through the Book Publishing Industry Development Program (BPIDP) for our publishing activities.

Key Porter Books Limited
70 The Esplanade
Toronto, Ontario
Canada M5E 1R2

www.keyporter.com

Text design: Peter Maher
Electronic formatting: Peter Maher

Printed and bound in Canada

04 05 06 07 08 09 6 5 4 3 2 1

For David, Dennis, Terry, Penny—DL

For John E. Sheppard, beau-père extraordinaire—MK

Contents

 So Cool

What's wrong with my body and everyone else so cool, so
super cool? But my
voice comes out like somebody squished a canary—or else, like a
bullfrog on steroids.
I hate my stupid voice. Also I hate my chest;
the thing just sits there, how can you get girls with a
pygmy chest like this?
Plus the zits, and the grebes, and they stare at you, they keep on
staring as if you
chose your own body on purpose—how do you get to be cool?
I'm like a one-man freak show.
If I was cool, I honestly wouldn't care.
But my body parts are a joke and I will never get them to grow the
     way I want to.

popping pimples in the park

We're popping pimples in the park,
Popping pimples after dark.

We pop them hot, we pop them cold,
We pop them when they're nine days old.

We pop them pink, we pop them yellow,
We pop them when they're fine and mellow.

We're soft-and-squeezy, over-easy,
Pimple-poppin' dandies!

Spell for Growing

Old momma teach me moonlight
Old momma teach me skin
Old momma teach me rhythm
When the ocean crashes in

And take me to the heartland
And teach me how to fear
Old momma teach me hunger
At the turning of the year

Old momma teach me music
Made of juniper and bone
Old momma teach me silence
In the certainty of stone.

Red Rover

I once had a dog and her name was Red Rover,
Stop here, or gently pass,
But where we played frisbee, the weeds have grown over,
And no one tends the grass.

The ground is all tangled with burdocks and clover,
And no one tends the grass,
And only one person still visits Red Rover,
Stop here, or gently pass.

Stop here or gently pass,
Stop here or gently pass,
Where burdocks and clover
Lie over Red Rover,
Beneath the cold cold grass.

Inspector Dogbone Gets His Man

I

Inspector Dogbone
  Is my name,
And catching bad guys
  Is my game.

I catch them high,
  I catch them low,
I catch them laughing
  Ho-ho-ho;

I catch them here,
  I catch them there,
I catch them in
  Their underwear.

I like to catch them
   By the toes,
Or by the moustache
   Or the nose;

From Corner Brook
   To Calgary
There's not a cop
   Can copy me—

'Cause every time
   I catch a crook,
I hang him up
   On a big brass hook.

Yet here I sit
   In the old Don Jail;
Come gather round,
   While I tell my tale.

II

One day, as I
    Was walking out,
I caught a bad guy
    By the snout.

He robbed a million-
    Dollar bank;
I grabbed his snout
    And gave a yank.

I grabbed his snoot
    And gave a flick,
But then he played
    A bad-guy trick.

His nose was nasty,
    Rough, and tough—
But with a snap
    He bit it off,

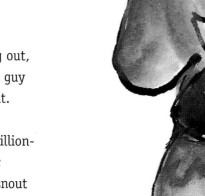

And just like that
    His smelly schnozz
Had vanished down
    His smelly jaws!

At once I grabbed him
    By the knee;
He ate that too,
    And laughed at me.

His back, his front,
    His head, his feet,
Whatever I seized
    The man would eat,

Till all there was
    Was just a mouth—
Which swallowed itself,
    And scampered south.

III

The case was gone!
  The case was gone!
The nose and the toes
  And the face were gone!

I had no crook,
  I had no crime,
But Dogbone's brain
  Worked overtime

And figured out
  A mighty plan
(For Dogbone always
  Gets his man).

Without a crime,
  Without a crook,
The only person
  Left to book

Was one whom I
  Had long suspected—
Inspector Dogbone,
  Whom I arrested.

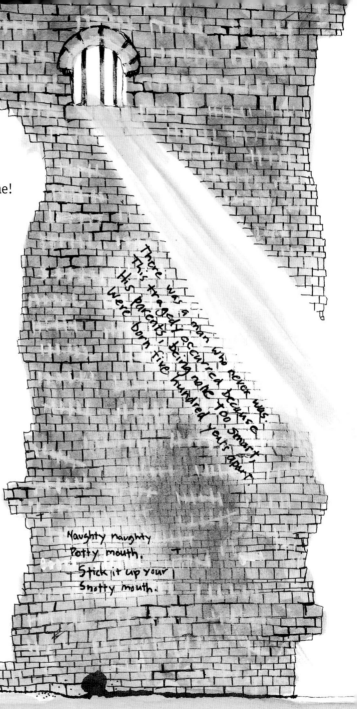

There was a man who never was.
This tragedy occurred because
His parents, being none too smart,
Were born five hundred years apart.

Naughty naughty
Potty mouth.
Stick it up your
Snotty mouth.

I didn't quake,
  I didn't quail,
I hauled his butt
  To the old Don Jail;

I threw that scumbag
  (Which was me)
In a stone cold cell
  And turned the key,

And here I sit
  Till the end of time,
Easing my soul
  With a Dogbone rhyme—

The victim of
  A bad guy's mouth,
Which swallowed itself,
  And scampered south.

But please recall
  As I rot in jail:
Inspector Dogbone
  Didn't fail.

And please remember
  If you can:
Inspector Dogbone
  Got his man!

Roses are rose
Liolets are plaid
Your underwear stinks
And your breath is bad

I wish I was a chocolate bar
upon a kitchen shelf.
I'd stop and stare, with loving care,
And then I'd eat myself!

Enough

A tongueful of
  Music,
A lungful of
  Air,
A handful of
  Friends
With a heartful to
  Spare—

If ever I lose
  The knack of wonder,
Just shovel a grave
  And dig me under.

High Summer

There's a sky so high you could live in it,
so blue you could
burrow an upside-down hole, and slide yourself in for keeps.

And sun like a honey rubdown
coating your face and skin, till you slowly remember
what bodies are for.

Blue lake; big sky; high lazy whiteout—
glory days.
Back in the city, let me be warmed for a year by the animal nudge of perfection.

Dorks from Outer Space

Dorks are coming,
Dorks are near,
Dorks invade
The atmosphere.

Dizzy dorks
In party hats,
Dumbbell dorks
With baseball bats,

In-line dorks
Who ram and slam,
On-line dorks
Like human spam,

Yakking dorks and
Dorkettes too,
Like a gabfest
At the zoo—

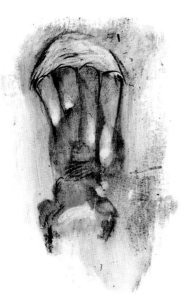

Dorks who ruin
Every story,
Dorks galore and
Dorks in glory!

Dorks have landed,
Dorks are here,
Dorks pollute
The atmosphere.

the museum of dirty minds

The stuff that goes on in my mind, I wouldn't
feed it to a pit bull.
Fry it up, you could use it for toxic waste.
There's stuff I can't even tell you—
garbage thoughts, incredible video scenes;
how does it get *in* there?

But there must be a Museum someplace for dirty minds. WORLD'S ALL-TIME
FREAKS AND PERVS AND MENTAL MISBEGOTTENS.
I could give it to them.
I'd leave this carton at the door, with breathing holes
and a typed-up note: "Please find enclosed
one dirty mind. Take good care of it—din-dins at
night, walkies if you remember—and oh by the way, kindly
strangle the filthy thing before it pollutes your museum."

That'll show my mind.
Then I'll take off down the lane—no
mind/no problem.

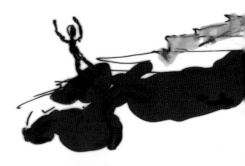

THE COMBAT

I stood there pushing, and
he stood there pushing, and
neither of us was gonna give in.

And my eyes were a brick wall, and
his eyes were a brick wall, and
neither one of us was gonna give in.

And to tell the truth, I can't remember now what the
fight was about—
some stupid thing.

But it felt good, because I never stood up to my father before.
So I pushed in my mind, and
he pushed in his mind, and there was

deadly combat between us. I was
scared, and brave, and alone—
I couldn't back down.

On that day of my life, something changed.
Whatever the fight was about, it wasn't *about* it;
I'm not even sure how it ended.

But this I knew: something deep had changed for keeps,
on that day when I stood there pushing, and my
Dad stood there pushing, and

neither one of us was ever gonna give in.

Pimples and Zits

Pimples and zits,
Pimples and zits,
We're painting our faces
With pimples and zits.

We wear them to movies,
We take them to school;
They're only pretend
But they look supercool—

'Cause who could help drooling
For zits on your face?
A chick without acne
Is just a disgrace!

And who wouldn't cream for
A spotty complexion?
The boys all go wild
For a pimple connection;

And then every night,
When we've thrilled them to bits,
We pull off the pimples
And peel off the zits.

The other Place

How come, when you're dozing through math, or hanging out
with your friends in the street after school, or drifting home, maybe
kicking a stone for luck—anyway, how come the world can just
stop?
     And you're into the other place, where
nothing has shape or a name:
just that funny electric blur, the space of waiting,
nothing to do but be there.
And you don't even want to be there—it just
takes you over, like it's where you belong.
What *is* it, the other place?
(Except when you're in it, you don't ask questions.)
I never told anybody this, but I'm telling you.
Do you sometimes feel like you're

gone,

gone,

gonzo in the brain?

Long Chant

One by water,
    Two by flame,
Three by the power
    Of the name;
Four by lightning,
    Five by hush,
In the bare and
    Burning bush;
Six by comrades,
    Seven alone,
Eight by the riddle
    In the stone;
Nine by vision,
    Ten by pain,
And the will
    To start again . . .

the pest

I feared the point had passed him by,
And so I sought to clarify:

"Your wits are dim, your talk is trite.
You are obnoxious to my sight."

I feared the point was not yet plain,
And so I laboured to explain:

"You are a clod, a total putz.
I loathe your palpitating guts."

I feared the point was still unclear,
And so I bellowed in his ear:

"I'd rather meet a bat from hell
Than breathe your nauseating smell!"

I feared the point remained in doubt,
And so I bopped him on the snout.

Children of Tomorrow

When first they came around me,
  I was baffled what to do.
Their outlines were in shadow,
  And the sounds were shadowed too.

But soon the figures clarified,
  And murmurs turned to words,
And as they spoke, my heart half-broke,
  For this is what I heard:

We are the children of tomorrow.
We are the ones who come behind.
Earth is a home that you have borrowed;
What home will we find?
What home will we find?

I like the way
You save on socks—
You wear them till
They're hard as rocks;
And I think those crooked
Teeth are keen—
Your mouth looks like
A slot machine
And every time
I see you grin
I stick another
Quarter in.
You make me laugh
Till we trip on chairs
One day we nearly
Fell downstairs—
Roses are red,
Violets are black,
If I was your mother
I'd give you back.
STOP THAT!

But still, you're kind of
Brave I guess,
Your **no** means**no**,
Your **yes** means **yes**

And even when
It makes you shrink,
You say the things
You truly think.

In fact your mouth
Is never closed;
Your tonsils blush
They're so exposed.

And your tweety voice
Is never quiet;
They must put birdseed
In your diet.

But still, you know
When we kid a lot
The time for kidding,
The time for not—

Get out of my face,
Get off of my case,
Or I'll murdelize you
From the human race

And let's hang out
In Kendal Park,
There's still an hour
Before it's dark;

'Cause some things last, and
Some things end —
I want you always
For my **friend**.

The Coat

I patched my coat with sunlight.
It lasted for a day.
I patched my coat with moonlight,
But the lining came away.
I patched my coat with lightning
And it flew off in the storm.
I patched my coat with darkness;
That coat has kept me warm.

Mister Cool

They call me Mister Cool,
The coolest dude in school.
My walk is cool, my talk is cool,
Because the cool shall rule.

So don't you be no fool,
No jackass or no mule;
Be smart, and you'll obey the rule—
Don't mess with Mister Cool!

The Proper Care of Silky Hair

The mighty mega-stegosaurus
Never takes the air
Without a length of dental floss
To groom its silky hair.

The noble reptile understands
The value of hygiene,
And labours long, with floss and song,
To keep its ringlets clean.

So come ye maidens in array,
And come ye lads in chorus:
Comb out the dross with dental floss,
And strut like stegosaurus.

French Kissing with Gum in Your Mouth

Say you're chomping this
giant wad of gum, and it's totally squishy. So you
grab this chick, and you french her smack on the kisser—
do your teeth stick together?
Or suppose one of you picks right then to launch the
world's biggest bubble—
does it blow up in*side* the other person?
Like, how does it actually work?
Kissing, I mean.
Do you have to ask her first?
What if your braces get locked—do the
cops come around with a blowtorch, and cut you apart?

See, I may not be ready for kissing. Even though I
like her, I like her a lot. She *knows* stuff, you can tell by that
faraway look she gets. And when she
breathes real slow, just breathes, and the air starts to
shimmer around her chest, like it's waiting for something,
I'm a goner. A total goner. I can
feel my mouth go dry, it's bye-bye brain, and when she
looks across at me, looking—oh man,
my stomach starts to cave in.

I like her so much. I don't know what to do.

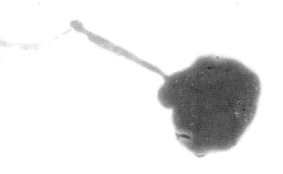

Sir Ethelred and the Fateful Tong

With that, the bold Sir Ethel sprang
And strung his bow with mighty twang
And swung his sword with mighty slang
And flung his tong with mighty flang,
   And yet the fling went wrong.

For ere Sir Ethel's fearsome flinging
Could send the foe to hellfire winging,
All in a bungled angle hanging
The fateful tong came boomeranging—
   And pronged him through the lung!

Now dong the gong with mournful bonging
For knights must die without belonging;
Young, young in years, with virtues thronging,
Pronged through the lung by a wrong-way tonging,
   The bold Sir Ethel is gone,
     Is gone,
   The brave Sir Ethel is gone.

The Mystery

Can't talk about it,
don't know if anybody else even feels it,
animals live in it, maybe they don't know it's there,
little kids the same;
grownups act oblivious—situation normal.
Half the time I just mooch along, then I laugh too loud.
But it catches me late at night, or in winter when
branches glow with snow against the bark, or some dumb old
song cracks me up and I want to go
howl in the city, or smash windows, or make my
life sheer shine in this miracle ache of a world.

Back When I Never Knew

Sometimes when the ache gets
too much, or my
friends start freaking and I'm not so cool myself,
or the whole world feels like it's sliding straight to ratshit—
sometimes I think back to a
bedtime long ago, I might have been four and my
mom still read to us; anyway, this one night
I stopped her, and I said the book out loud,
word for word, page-turn for page-turn, and it was
cool, it was perfect, it was all
pretend because the thing is, I still couldn't read.
But I was racing to big-kid freedom, just
chasing my runaway heart; I was chugging to paradise, to
light in the grown-up world—coronas of
freefall light in the fever and stations of growing. And I knew,
wherever I went, my mom would always be there . . .

Oh man, sometimes when the ache gets too much I
think back to then, back when I was so
hot to be older, and everything big was golden,
and the brand new world was waiting to show me secrets—
back when I never knew; I just
never knew.

The House of Alone

You want lonely, we got lonely.
You want sad, there's sad to the bone.
Any time you feel like hurting
Just come on down to the House of Alone.

Come to where it's half past heartache.
Come to where we feel the pain.
You can leave the way you entered,
But you know you'll come again.

It hurts to see how bad they hurt you.
It hurts to hear you moan and groan.
Just knock three times and you'll be welcome;
There's room to spare in the House of Alone.

So come on down and ease your weary.
Come on home and taste the blues.
No one here has found the answer,
But we've saved a place for you.

You know you'll leave the house by morning.
You know you'll cry and then go home.
But any time your heart starts hurting
There's always room in the House of Alone.

VACANCY

INSTRUCTIONS

Kindly take a number,
Kindly join the queue,
Kindly wait in line, while we
Suggest what you could do;
    It goes like this—

**"First you take a number,
Then you join the queue,
Then you stand in line, while we
Decide what you must do;
    It goes like this—**

*'Take a lousy number,
Join the stupid queue,
Stand in line, and do not whine,
And here is what you'll do;
    It goes like this—*

"YOU NEVER TOOK A NUMBER!
YOU NEVER JOINED THE QUEUE!
GET BACK IN LINE, YOU SCABBY SWINE,
OR HERE IS WHAT WE'LL DO
    TO PUNISH YOU;
        IT GOES LIKE THIS—... ""

Curse and Farewell

I won't go quiet at the bell
I won't go easy into hell
I'm not your pooch to buy and sell
I don't believe the lies you tell

I've got an itchy little fuse
I've got a gale force in my shoes
I've got a supersonic force
I've got a strike and no remorse

You're not the captain of my dream
You're not the coffee in my cream
So when your crummy life is through
Don't come to me to comfort you

I got a strike and no remorse
I got a supersonic force
I won't go quiet at the bell
I won't go easy into hell

Me and the Ultimate Sensual Experience

What can I tell you? Paradise gets leaky;
me too, and then you
wake up totally goobered. Stuck to your pj's.
Thing is, this is supposed to be the #1 thrill of your life,
and every time, I sleep through it.
If they had a contest on TV—"Tell Us Your
Ultimate Sensual Experience"—
I'd finish last.
"Umm . . . don't ask me. I was out like a light."

My *ultimate sensual experience*. Man, it's weird.
Maybe it's better with somebody else. But for now
it's this mystery place I go to, and then nothing but
leftover ecstasy stains. Some
absentee whiff.

Still, it's kind of cool, I guess—being a man and all.

THE HERO'S GRAVE

The wind was going crazy
With tons and tons of rain,
When me and my dog Blackie
Came tearing down the lane

And set out for the safehouse
In Rosenbury Road,
Where brave resistance fighters
Were waiting for the code.

And Blackie ran like kingdom come,
And I ran close behind,
While rocket-launchers lit the sky
And almost lit my mind,

For soldiers from the Tyrant's guard
Were firing at a bus;
I checked for burnt-out tenements
In case they spotted us.

Then on we ran, and on we ran,
And on we ran again
Past lines of refugees, who trudged
Like phantoms in the rain,

And in my mind, I held the code
In secrecy and need;
I knew, if I could reach that house,
The city could be freed—

The passwords could be synchronized,
A false one scrambled in,
And at the stroke of twelve o'clock
The rising would begin.

More soldiers blocked the passage now
And guns began to bark,
Till Blackie found an alleyway
That circled through the dark—

But then a bullet ricocheted
And downed him in the street;
I picked him up and carried him
The final hundred feet.

I whistled at the cellar door.
It opened silently.
I told the men the code—and, yes,
The rest is history:

Our fighters moved from block to block
With courage and with speed,
And by the time the sun was up
The city had been freed.

But that was years and years ago;
The Tyrant rules no more,
And I can barely recognize
The legends of the war.

But when my children ask about
The night I brought the code,
I lead them to the hero's grave
In Rosenbury Road.

Living the Life

Hickory dickory
Slippery dock,
When I was new, I was
Nothing o'clock.

Hickory dickory
Slippery den,
When I am gone, I'll be
Nothing again.

Hickory dickory
Slippery dive—
Isn't it something, to
Be alive?!

What I Learned in Math Today

Okay, that math class changed my life—
but maybe I was
never *me* at all. I could be
someone I never met, a human mutant;
how would I know?
All I know is, at this exact instant—at 2:42, on Tuesday—
the rush inside me feels (hang on) like a
hiccup in actual space, I'm
hopping & bopping like a
pinball machine from Mars, my
mind keeps doing
bungee jumps oh man I can't
believe the way she looked at me in math!

the shame

Among the thousand, or maybe the million things I know,
my all-time least favourite is this:
how shitty it feels, when you admire somebody
for their talent, or guts, or maybe just their
funny way of getting through the day; anyway, as
I keep trying not to tell you, how shitty it feels when you
admire this person, and then some mean-
minded jerkoff starts badmouthing them behind their back,
and instead of sticking up for them—and
remember, this friend has never done anything to hurt you—
you just stand there, while the cracks and cheap laughs get
meaner and hey you laugh too and
then, god help me I did I
joined in the trash brigade, I got off this
killer put-down, we all cracked up we were howling we were
helpless with laughter and I walked away down the hall I was
caving in, I hated them all and myself I wanted to
break something, I walked and walked I felt so
helpless with shame, with the
shame.

Rainy Day Night

Creeks all run to the river
river runs to the sea
but nobody runs
nobody runs
nobody runs to me.

Hush you little darling
hush your sad refrain
the sky must weep, and you must sleep,
and ache away the pain.

Who Cans Toucans?

Now I can can, and you can can,
But Jan can can more than anybody else can:
Cans of bran and cans of flan—
Till Jan made plans to can pecans.

And the plan was pretty canny, for Jan's old granny
Helped her pickle those pecans, jamming every nook and cranny.
First she canned them on the weekends, cramming wee cans full of pecans,
Using two hard-working toucans who could pack a can a day.

And it was *one* can, *two* cans, *three* cans of pecans . . .
But Jan's Can Plan spanned as far as she could see cans.
So she bought a big machine for packing wee cans full of pecans,
And she taught the toucans to can cans as fast as cans can *be* canned.

But a toucan can't can pecans if the pickle mixture's sticking,
And the faster those poor toucans canned, the more the pickle thickened;
Soon the cans were flying past her, faster than the birds could master,
For two toucans can't can three cans in a one-pecan-can span.

Still the cans flew fast and faster, till Jan's toucans faced disaster,
While the big machine kept shrieking like a manic ghetto-blaster;
Jan could see cans leaking pecans, toucans tweaking one-two-three cans,
Till at last, aghast, she spied two cans of new-canned toucan pie . . .

Very lowly, very slowly, Jan destroyed the canner wholly,
And she raised a mighty monument beneath the clear blue sky.
It declared, *"Here lie two toucans, clad in two cans meant for pecans.*
I lived to can; they died by can; let no one can again."

QUIZ

What gets you through the day?
Your best friend, being there.

What gets you through the night?
The music, breathing your secret name in the dark.

What are the seven conditions of lonely?
No friend, no joke, no touch, no dream of a better world, no baffled
    abiding parents, no right or wrong, no earth surviving.

What must you give to find the way?
The rest of your life.

Night Thanks

Lightfall to
  Nightfall, the
Earth settles
  Deep,
Hunkering
  Down in a
Blanket of
  Sleep.

Careload by
  Heartload, the
World falls
  Away.
Tomorrow's
  Tomorrow;
Be glad for
  Today.

DEEPER

Often at night, sometimes
out in the snow or going into the music, the voice says,
"Deeper."
I don't know what it means.
Just, "Push it. Go further. Go deeper."
And when they come talking at me I get
antsy at times, but always the voice keeps saying:
"That is not it. Go deeper."
There is danger in this, also
breakaway hunches and I believe it can issue in
flickers of homing; but I
cannot control it, all I know is the one thing—
"Deeper. You must go further. You must go deeper."